Gratitude Haiku

Gratitude Haiku

Rae Berg

ELYSSAR PRESS
Redlands, CA

Printed in the United States of America

First Printing, 2024
ISBN 979-8-9898850-0-8

Elyssar Press
175 Bellevue Ave
Redlands, CA 92373

www.ElyssarPress.com

Cover photograph by Rae Berg
Cover and book design by Stephanie Aoun Bou Karam
All photographs by the author, and are used with appropriate permissions.
Image by rawpixel.com

Contents

Welcome, reader!

This book is both a gift and an invitation, created in the midst of our generation's biblical-like plague, where haiku became for many an angel of mercy.

A gift to you:

From me, a happily-retired pastor who, in thirty-five years of ministry, preached from various pulpits an excess of two million words, and now am drawn to the "less is more" life. In all sorts of ways, this philosophy permeates my being, my decisions, and my weeks.

During the pandemic, I began writing haiku. A story in seventeen syllables. If a poem is a dandelion, the haiku is one single fluff of a dandelion. Each haiku, just a spare three lines beginning with five syllables, adding seven syllables, and concluding with five syllables.

This book contains many such seventeen-syllable gifts, accompanied by my own photography–most of which was created during the pandemic and collected into one package. You'll notice that nothing is capitalized in these haiku. My intention is to create a level playing field between the various characters, images, and ideas. Punctuation is sparse, so as to not distract from your interpretations of the haiku, with the following intent: a colon suggests contemplative connections or bridges built into the haiku; a period denotes a thoughtful pause, an invitation to breathe and ponder; and a comma indicates a brief, gentle pause, accompanied by a warm embrace. Question marks and the occasional exclamation point demonstrate, as you would imagine, queries and excitement. Some of these haiku are grouped nontraditionally into a handful to tell a story using a few more words.

Accompanying each haiku is an unspoken invitation to ponder the words or gaze at the photo, and find inspiration to write your own seventeen-syllable gift, a moment in time describing your unique experience.

An invitation from life:

Anyone can write seventeen syllables.
Even you.
Yes, I know...
I didn't believe it either when told the same.
Think brief, not small. Settle yourself in some part of the natural world. Look at the veins of a fallen autumn leaf for starters. Or gaze into the irises of a beloved. Describe that experience, that moment, in only one or two words. Attach that word to another, creating a thought. Let that thought lead you to one or two others, as you stay in the moment of the experience. A type of stepping stone exercise... one present step at a time. You will arrive at the magical three lines that shimmer your momentary experience onto the page.

Author, teacher, and haiku master Clark Strand said that at its most basic, a haiku is whatever you can get away with in seventeen syllables. One of my writing colleagues, Margaret Roark, upon invitation to write haiku, took Mr. Strand's more rebellious path a step further. Instead of the traditional three lines, she writes one full sentence, seventeen syllables total. Allen Ginsberg is said to have created this form of haiku, dubbed the American sentence.

In this book, I join them in suggesting there are no poetry police and no writing regulations. There is only a clear invitation from life whose heart beats in yours and says in countless voices, "Yes, yes you can!"

Gratitudes

With any project, no creative soul is an island... especially in a pandemic. I am grateful to the following people:

Rev. Judith Favor, my most recent writing teacher, who reintroduced me to haiku; my colleagues in the online, pandemic-inspired Contemplative Listening & Writing retreat which spanned all of 2021; Spirituality & Practice who dared and dreamed this writing opportunity into reality amid a pandemic; all those who told me, long ago and more recently, "you have good eye for photography;" professional photographers who have complimented, and thus encouraged, my camera work; teachers Natalie Goldberg and Clark Strand, who introduced me to Bashō, Chiyo-ni, Buson, Issa, and Shiki—haiku ancestors;
Katia Hage, my friend and publisher—and her team at Elyssar Press—who had the courage to tell me my initial haiku "held promise;" and finally and heartfully, my family—chosen and born—you know who you are and what you mean to my life.

Thank you to everyone who helped bring this precious sprinkling of words and photographs to life.
Grateful.
Very grateful.

one

Spring

Author's home and neighborhood, San Bernardino Mountains, California

it started with tea
daily. morning. sometimes cream.
this calm in lockdown

Author's home and neighborhood, San Bernardino Mountains, California

a cloth of beauty
masking breath, warding danger
how many we need

California Botanic Garden, Claremont, California

clever cacti breathe
a moment of levity
into covid's fear

Author's home and neighborhood, San Bernardino Mountains, California

pathway of stone shows
where to walk if you want to
walk within the lines

Author's home and neighborhood, San Bernardino Mountains, California

SPRING

come away awhile
brrr. too cold for human skin
if tree stumps could talk

Author's home and neighborhood, San Bernardino Mountains, California

SPRING

stencils of pine trees
drawn white by last night's ice storm
nature's art displayed

Author's home and neighborhood, San Bernardino Mountains, California

snow panorama
a whole forest of water
fresh for the drinking

a theology of incarnation

within the divine
spirit's shadow excludes none
love incarnated

humans born of earth
placed in beauty as our home
pulse with divine breath

trees, plants, animals
humans, seasons, stone, earth, air
enlivened with god

anger, sadness, joy
grief, frustration, fatigue, sleep
dance with the goddess

what a difference
divine-within-all matters
making holy now

one

Summer

The Living Desert Zoo and Gardens, Palm Desert, California

giraffe silhouette
and majestic mountain frame
stand in solitude

Author's home and neighborhood, San Bernardino Mountains, California

rocks swirling with life
maps of water now long dried
echo in stillness

Author's home and neighborhood, San Bernardino Mountains, California

dewdrops of mercy
spill compassion on the world
gentle sure quan-yin

Author's home and neighborhood, San Bernardino Mountains, California

summer's first iris
translucent in the sunshine
beauty pageant queen

Author's home and neighborhood, San Bernardino Mountains, California

healing souls are joined
a broken vessel repaired
to hold love enough

Author's home and neighborhood, San Bernardino Mountains, California

crystal bowls quiver
with vibrations for healing
change chaos to calm

Huntington Library and Gardens, San Marino, California

morning glories reach
to enfold your nearby nose
with sweet aroma

Huntington Library and Gardens, San Marino, California

falling rushing sheer
as the backside of water
still nourishes thirst

Huntington Library and Gardens, San Marino, California

from the redwood's base
comes its genetic future
life from the ground up

Old Mission Garden, Santa Barbara, California

leaves upon leaves poised
turning skilled sponges upward
wait for rain to fall

Author's home and neighborhood, San Bernardino Mountains, California

SUMMER

from confused brambles
grow brilliant red rose signposts
each year without fail

Author's home and neighborhood, San Bernardino Mountains, California

christmas cactus or
sometimes easter or summer
each day a party

one

Autumn

an oak tree survives
though blaze and smoke seared its soul
we are home again

Author's home and neighborhood, San Bernardino Mountains, California

el dorado fire
bravely stopped one block away
please no more reveals

Author's home and neighborhood, San Bernardino Mountains, California

Author's home and neighborhood, San Bernardino Mountains, California

acorns from the oak
abundant carpet of food
why do humans hoard?

Author's home and neighborhood, San Bernardino Mountains, California

who owns the forest?
who dares drill a wound into
sentient being's skin?

Author's home and neighborhood, San Bernardino Mountains, California

green chair sits alone
looking out on the mountain
dying oak leaf joins

Author's home and neighborhood, San Bernardino Mountains, California

abandoned snow sled
memories melted its path
a sadness lingers

Author's home and neighborhood, San Bernardino Mountains, California

scene of covid calm:
a toast to safety and home
nothing neat at all

Author's home and neighborhood, San Bernardino Mountains, California

palm tree seems unfazed
by the approaching storm clouds
rooted as she is

Old Mission Garden, Santa Barbara, California

a tower of stone
marks the place where four friendships
became team goddess

Cambria, California

bird perched on a twig
sings a lullaby while earth's
largest ocean rests

Cambria, California

everyday a path
walking our way to our core
one step at a time

Labyrinth, St. Barnabas Episcopal Church, Borrego Springs, California

where does daylight go
must travel in clouds to make
a sky quilt of warmth

Clinton, Oklahoma

one

Winter

living through covid
with photographs and humor
how have you survived

Uranus Fudge Factory, Uranus, Missouri

illusive. hidden.
spontaneous and playful
this thing we call joy

unbidden it comes
waiting to transform shadows
to the yet unseen

Private home, Eugene, Oregon

we are tired covid
"go away, come back, go 'way"
when your work is done

Author's home and neighborhood, San Bernardino Mountains, California

coronavirus
nature seems done with humans
no more second chance

we have mucked it up
fossil fuels trash gluttony
greed pride envy sloth

waste too near our tent
wise father said long ago
dare we ask: forgive?

Death Valley, California

birds squirrels chipmunks
ev'ryone is skitterish
weather's coming in

Author's home and neighborhood, San Bernardino Mountains, California

bud of the oak tree
shyly hidden at twig's end
life silhouetted

Author's home and neighborhood, San Bernardino Mountains, California

casts a long shadow
this tiny pinecone is tall
in winter sunset

Author's home and neighborhood, San Bernardino Mountains, California

what is the color of life
vinca asks of winter's chill
catch me if you can

Author's home and neighborhood, San Bernardino Mountains, California

manzanita shines
in winter's sunsetting light
see you tomorrow!

Author's home and neighborhood, San Bernardino Mountains, California

two

Spring

Wildlife Safari, Winston, Oregon

a mother never
stops giving birth to new life
pain to joy once more

Wildlife Safari, Winston, Oregon

Huntington Library and Gardens, San Marino, California

earth now is wailing
with the world in my bloodstream
i dare put down roots

Note: Thanks for the poem "With the World in My Bloodstream," by Thomas Merton, which he wrote while he was convalescing from back surgery after falling deeply in love with the attending hospital nurse. The poem's title here refers to falling in love with Earth.

Author's home and neighborhood, San Bernardino Mountains, California

Author's home and neighborhood, San Bernardino Mountains, California

two signs of springtime
hummer's food on the menu
daffodil not quite

Author's home and neighborhood, San Bernardino Mountains, California

mists of avalon
without the travel and cost
still cloud my vision

Author's home and neighborhood, San Bernardino Mountains, California

SPRING

springtime blooms yellow
as daffodils dare to rise
born of winter's chill

Author's home and neighborhood, San Bernardino Mountains, California

shimmering in sun
lightened by separation
fallen pine branch waves

Author's home and neighborhood, San Bernardino Mountains, California

snow outlined oak tree
no grievance heard within as
branches lean sunward

Author's home and neighborhood, San Bernardino Mountains, California

sweet tinkling bamboo
gently chimes to soothe the souls
attacked by terror

Note: This photograph was taken on January 9, 2021, three days after the domestic terror attack on the US Capitol Building and its government employees, elected and appointed.

Reche Canyon, California

SPRING

while the others graze
i'm all ears and flared nostrils
said wild ass close by

Author's home and neighborhood, San Bernardino Mountains, California

SPRING ————————————————————

mind full of noise as
leprechauns play with steel wool
covid leftovers

Redlands, California

a sky full of stars
comes to ground in morning light
twinkling in these stones

Huntington Library and Gardens, San Marino, California

SPRING

tender young rosebud
hidden waiting to appear
winter's gift to spring

two

Summer

Masonic Cemetery, McMinnville, Oregon

breathe in earth. stand firm.
still. quiet. observer. breathe
out what does not serve

Redlands, California

SUMMER

compassion met me
in "the real" of my distress
held me till it passed

Private home, Eugene, Oregon

death comes to each door
ev'ry stem, tree, sentient
and yet still we wail

Hendricks Park, Eugene, Oregon

body aches for care
from extremities inward
in this moment, choice

Author's home and neighborhood, San Bernardino Mountains, California

a pandemic pause:
afternoon with fava beans
shucked boiled soaked peeled gone

Madera, California

olive tree in fruit
one of many sour acres
no tasting just yet

Wildlife Safari, Winston, Oregon

a good hair day looks
something like this and nothing
like this in covid

Wildlife Safari, Winston, Oregon

this way. that way. where
to go for food and water
emus on parade

Private home, McMinnville, Oregon

————————————

just because a flag
claims something or another
doesn't make it so

Point Arena, California

flamingo flowers
in breezy community
stand to pray for us

Fort Ross State Historic Park, California

windswept western coast
a perfect dance floor choice of
pink flamingo grass

Del Mar, California

breathe in evening air
pathway of light on water
hush, child, day is done

two

Autumn

half full? half empty?
a cup is refillable
always. daily. now.

Author's home and neighborhood, San Bernardino Mountains, California

breath and forgiveness
both move as wind flowing free
loosening grief's grip

Cambria, California

faraway mountains
yawning night into color
light peeks then hits snooze

this beloved day
starts slowly and leisurely
waking with each breath

Sunrise over Barstow, California

trees stand alert while
pandemic grocery shopping
fresh breath of beauty

Interlaken Shopping Center, Yucaipa, California

variegated leaves
attached still to their fall tree
not ready to drop

Worcester, Massachusetts

autumnal engine
fired up for season's labor
birthing winter soon

Worcester, Massachusetts

yellow spring again
a half year later this time
falling soon to earth

Worcester, Massachusetts

ground of all being
catches the leaf as it falls
to a soft future

Worcester, Massachusetts

driving cross-country
signs of exclusivity
randomly appear

Miami, Oklahoma

pandemic campus
learning portals have no need
of blue chairs in shade

Illinois College, Jacksonville, Illinois

energy of earth
wind and fire in the night sky
power a new day

Paw Paw, Illinois

two

Winter

an event canceled
better than a life canceled
omicron christmas

Note: With thanks to Dr. Tedros Adhanom Ghebreyesus, Director General of the World Health Organization (WHO) and his cautionary words of instruction delivered on December 21, 2021.

Author's home and neighborhood, San Bernardino Mountains, California

the plague skulks through us
elders, young, sickly, stubborn
covid passover

Author's home and neighborhood, San Bernardino Mountains, California

this morning more light
see the horizon's promise
light returns, always

stones speak in shadow
"through the threshold of bluestones
light returns, always"

we see with our eyes
feel coursing in bones and veins
light returns, always

Screenshots, via English Heritage

over in eire
for as many centuries
light returns, always

on circular stone
triple spiral ancient art
light returns, always

down darkened passage
as midwinter dawns again
light returns, always

Screenshots, via Newgrange, Government of Ireland

from covid's long weight
with choked voice, her tears restrained
our guide promises:

"everything passes—
monument newgrange teaches
resilience remains!"

now the new year turns
now hope bears her sacred fruit
blessed solstice light!

Note: The haiku on pages 172-177 are written based on witnessing the Onscreen Solstice Sunrise at Stonehenge and Newgrange on December 22, 2021. All photographs are computer screenshots, used with permission of English Heritage, Stonehenge and Office of Public Works, Government of Ireland, Newgrange.

Footage courtesy of Alan Betson, The Irish Times

Screenshot, via Newgrange, Government of Ireland

knowing with the heart
emmanuel, yes, comes down
but also comes forth

Note: This poem is inspired by the final of the seven "O Antiphons" podcast, Advent 2021, by Diana Butler Bass, and also by the poem "Psalm of an Emerging Emmanuel" by Edward Hays.

California Botanic Garden, Claremont, California

three

Spring

Author's home and neighborhood, San Bernardino Mountains, California

SPRING ————————————————————————

go sit in your cell
it will teach you ev'rything
see clouds in my tea

Note: Gratitude to Desert Abba Moses the Black and Thich Nhat Hanh, respectively, for the verbal images "sit in your cell" and "clouds in my tea." Both of these phrases are found throughout their teachings.

Author's home and neighborhood, San Bernardino Mountains, California

continuation
as the rain is of the cloud
so am I of life

awaken again
to love from love enfolding
continuation

Note: Ideas in this haiku are inspired by the book, *No Death, No Fear*, by Thich Nhat Hanh, my continuing teacher.

Author's home and neighborhood, San Bernardino Mountains, California

a birthday haiku:
migraine gone, walk in forest
grateful to be born

Florence, Oregon

five things that matter:
i love you. forgive you. thanks.
forgive me. goodbye.

Note: This haiku was inspired by an online webinar on August 20, 2020, entitled "Grief & Loss," sponsored by the United Church of Christ National Office.

Private home, McMinnville, Oregon

A Haiku-inspired Epitaph

pause only a bit
to sing me songs and
tell me stories and
laugh with me again
in my season of dying

then go, live your life
leave death enshrouded,
darkened magic space,
cyclically to rise again
life and death conjoined

A Final Blessing

bless to us this love
deepening, fluid, present
as the air and ground

bless to us this love
in and of community
born in wombs of light

bless to us this love
compassion incarnated
through listening ears

bless to us this love
for today and tomorrow
without and within

* amen and blessed be *

Author's home and neighborhood, San Bernardino Mountains, California

SPRING ─────────────────────────────

she sits and wonders
"shading the dust from her eyes"
much still to be learned

Note: Thanks to Natalie Goldberg's book *Three Simple Lines: A Writer's Pilgrimage into the Heart and Homeland of Haiku*, for teaching that the quoted line is the Zen way of saying "seeing clearly" (Goldberg, 5).

About the author

Rae Berg is the chosen pen name of Rev. Dr. Sharon Rae Graff, composed of her given middle name, Rae, from her paternal Welsh and Irish roots, and from her maternal grandmother's family name, Berg, representing her Norwegian and German heritage. Berg refers to mountain and holds special meaning since the author has lived in the southern California mountains for over twenty years with her spouse.

She earned a bachelor's degree of science (BS) from Bushnell University, a master's degree of education (MA) from the Claremont School of Theology, and a doctorate in ministry (DMin) from the San Francisco Theological Seminary. As an ordained pastor in the United Church of Christ, Rae Berg served several congregations and nonprofits throughout her career. Now in retirement, she has trained as a certified sound healer and spiritual coach, and has moved from her practice of writing weekly sermons, reports, and prayers to the more focused and abbreviated form of haiku.

Not formally trained in haiku, her attempts in this—her first book—are novice and flavored with hope that the reader will be inspired to give haiku a go!

For Further Reading and Enjoyment of Haiku

Goldberg, Natalie. *Three Simple Lines: A Writer's Pilgrimage into the Heart and Homeland of Haiku.* Novato: New World Library, 2021.

Saigyō. *Gazing at the Moon: Buddhist Poems of Solitude.* McKinney, Meredith, translator. Boulder: Shambhala Publications, Inc., 2021.

Strand, Clark. *Seeds from a Birch Tree: (25th Anniversary Edition: Revised & Expanded, 2023) Writing Haiku and the Spiritual Journey.* New York: Hyperion, 1997.

Strand, Clark. Instagram: @ClarkStrand. Posts of haiku with accompanying photographs.